A SUMMARY & ANALYSIS OF DORIS KEARNS GOODWIN'S

A SUMMARY & ANALYSIS OF DORIS KEARNS GOODWIN'S

TEAM OF RIVALS
LINCOLN

THE POLITICAL GENIUS OF ABRAHAM LINCOLN

by

SAVE TIME SUMMARIES

i

Note to Readers: We encourage you to first order a copy of Doris Kearns Goodwin's full book, _Team of Rivals: The Political Genius of Abraham Lincoln_ before you read this unofficial Book Summary & Review.

Other Amazon Kindle Ebooks from _Save Time Summaries:_

Summary of Mark Owen's _No Easy Day: The Firsthand Account of the Mission That Killed Osama Bin Laden_

Summary of Dr. Eben Alexander's _Proof of Heaven: A Neurosurgeon's Journey Into the Afterlife_

Summary of Stephen Covey's _The 7 Habits of Highly Effective People_

Save Time Summaries
Las Vegas, NV 89128
savetimesummaries@gmail.com

Table of Contents

OVERVIEW

Team of Rivals: The Political Genius of Abraham Lincoln is not a simple tale about a simple man. The book offers an in-depth look into the mind of Abraham Lincoln as well as those who would support and oppose him. In order to know Lincoln, one must know his friends and enemies as well.

Though *Team of Rivals* could be classified as a biography, it is so much more. The reader learns about the history of the United States, the lifestyle differences of the 19th century, and the atrocities of war that is fought on their own soil. However, there is still more in *Team of Rivals* that is useful to anyone who is placed in a position of leadership. Lincoln was not afraid of opposing viewpoints. Indeed, he sought them out. Before making decisions with far-reaching implications, he had consulted with every person he respected and some that he did not. He knew when to back away and when to hold tight. He also knew the value of well-crafted words in spite of the fact that he was never formally educated.

Team of Rivals takes the reader through Lincoln's early days, his failed romance with

Ann Rutledge, his marriage to Mary Todd, and his career and political aspirations. The book does more than that as well. The reader also learns the details about each of Lincoln's opponents and how each one would become vital to his presidency and, ultimately, the fate of the nation.

ABOUT THE AUTHOR of *TEAM OF RIVALS*

"Doris Kearns Goodwin (born Doris Helen Kearns; January 4, 1943) is a Pulitzer Prize-winning American biographer, historian, and an oft-seen political commentator. She is the author of biographies of several U.S. Presidents, including *Lyndon Johnson and the American Dream*; *The Fitzgeralds and the Kennedys: An American Saga*; *No Ordinary Time: Franklin and Eleanor Roosevelt* (which won the Pulitzer Prize for History in 1995); and her most recent book, *Team of Rivals: The Political Genius of Abraham Lincoln*." (Wikipedia.com)

PART I: THE RIVALS
CHAPTER 1: FOUR MEN WAITING

Summary

The ballot for the Republican Party's presidential nominee was to be decided on May 18, 1860. Four men were vying for that title. William Henry Seward was the likeliest choice. Being the governor of New York, Seward was so certain of his nomination that he had already proudly written a valedictory speech by that May day. Ohio Governor Salmon P. Chase was also a contender. Seward viewed Chase as his primary competitor in this race for the highest office. Seward troubled over his competitor due to Chase's extensive political experience in his role as governor and in the United States Senate. Edward Bates also had a long political career. He had served in the United States House of Representatives for Missouri and spent time in the Senate for that state as well. During his time as a hopeful nominee, Bates was Missouri's attorney general. Though Seward was the favorite, any of the three were reasonable choices for the Republican Party. None thought of the fourth man, Abraham Lincoln, as a true opponent. Lincoln was an Illinois lawyer who had served only one term in Congress more than 10 years earlier. Though he was well known by all as an excellent orator, he was not taken seriously by the other three men.

KEY TAKE-AWAYS

- Lincoln was considered to be the underdog in the 1860 presidential election.
- Each of Lincoln's rivals was more politically seasoned and therefore more likely to win the nomination.

CHAPTER 2: THE LONGING TO RISE

Summary

Each of the four men had his share of ups and downs in his early life. William Henry Seward grew up in a comfortable, slave-owning family. Unlike most slave-owners, the Sewards allowed the children to spend time with the slaves. They also gave the slave's children access to education. This gave Seward an appreciation for the slaves as people rather than property. Seward graduated from Union College with honors, and then joined the legal profession. He passed the bar in New York and joined a firm at the age of 23, at which time he also wed Frances Miller.

Salmon Portland Chase was also part of a distinguished family. Three generations of the Chase family lived in Cornish, New Hampshire where Chase was born and raised. However, at the age of seven, Chase's father invested in a glass factory, which resulted in bankruptcy. Chase's father soon died. Salmon was sent to live with an uncle who was president of Cincinnati College. Ever the intellectual "prodigy," Chase enrolled as a freshman at age 13. At 15, Chase was admitted at Dartmouth. He graduated with honors by the time he was 19. Like Seward, Chase joined the legal profession, working as a counsel for financial institutions in Cincinnati. Meanwhile, he was married to Catherine Garniss, who gave birth to a daughter also named Catherine. While his wife died in childbirth, Catherine the daughter passed only five years later. Chase's second wife was Eliza Ann Smith. She gave birth to daughters Kate and Eliza, the second of whom died at birth. Chase's second wife died from tuberculosis not long after. Chase's third wife was Sarah Belle Ludlow. Like his two previous wives, Sarah died young as did the second of the two daughters she begat. Chase then decided not to remarry as he served as a single father to his two surviving daughters, Kate and Nettie.

Edward Bates was a Virginian but left home at a young age. He joined forces during the War of 1812 and, two years later, settled in Missouri. His brother, Frederick, had just been appointed as Secretary of the territory by Thomas Jefferson. Bates, with the help of his brother, practiced law in St. Louis. He and his colleague Joshua Barton created a practice that represented some of the most well-known, respected, and powerful men in the area.

Lincoln's obstacles are well known and documented. His experiences were opposite those of his rivals for the 1860 election. Lincoln was born to a very poor family in Kentucky; his father could neither read nor write. Whereas his rivals were from large families, Lincoln's brother and sister died young, leaving him an only child. Little is known about Lincoln's mother, Nancy Hanks. It has been noted that she was intelligent. It was she who taught Lincoln to read, but she died when Lincoln was only nine years old. Lincoln, therefore, was unable to have any sort of education because the schools in Kentucky required a tuition payment that the elder Lincoln could not afford. Lincoln taught himself, reading from the Bible, Aesop's Fables, Shakespeare, and the Revised Statutes of Indiana, which contained copies of the United States Constitution and the Declaration of Independence. Lincoln, like all others, was interested in practicing law, but he did so without the advantages his competitors had. He also faced tragedy when his first love, Ann Rutledge, who died from typhoid at age 22.

KEY TAKE-AWAYS

- Lincoln's background was vastly different from that of his competitors. Each of the others had some family money and connections that aided them in their pursuit of law and eventual political office.
- Death and mourning were commonplace in the 19th century and quite prevalent in the lives of each of the four men.

CHAPTER 3: THE LURE OF POLITICS

Summary

The country was still new during the early 19th century. Intelligent men distinguished themselves by pursuing political careers. The four men would find their way into politics in varied ways. Bates was drawn more to a family life in Missouri than to a political future in Washington. Though he pursued and lost a U.S. Senate bid, he seemed to be relieved at the loss so that he could spend more time with his wife and growing family. Conversely, Seward seemed to prefer his political career and advanced rapidly on behalf of his beloved Whig party. Lincoln had less success than the others, though he did pursue his political career adamantly. While chasing his political dreams, he married Mary Todd. This was an act that he did, at times, believe would hinder his political aspirations. Indeed, he ended the engagement repeatedly before ultimately committing to the marriage. Chase was the least politically motivated of the three. He found himself in the public eye when he physically blocked an angry mob from storming the offices of the *Philanthropist*, an abolitionist newspaper. Along with his writings that decried slavery, this affair spurred Chase to pursue political office. Though he had some early strife, he would eventually become a U.S. senator and governor of Ohio.

KEY TAKE-AWAY

- Political careers served as the ultimate proof of intelligence and power in the early 19th century.

CHAPTER 4: PLUNDER AND CONQUEST

Summary

Abraham Lincoln's one and only term in Congress began in 1847. Coincidentally, when Lincoln moved to Washington with his wife, the United States was embroiled in the Mexican-American War. Lincoln, still a Whig at that time, adamantly and loudly opposed the war. His very vocal opposition gave some of his supporters a reason to admire him. Many others felt that he was overly boisterous in his disapproval of President James K. Polk, particularly as a freshman congressman. Indeed, this was thought by most to be the end of his political career and nearly was. However, there was much more than the argument against or for the Mexican-American War at stake. After the Treaty of Guadalupe Hidalgo on February 2, 1848, the United States acquired new land. Lincoln and his future rivals fought against allowing slavery in these soon-to-be states. Unfortunately for Lincoln, he would have to do so from his law offices in Springfield. When his term in Congress ended, that would be the last of his in-office political career until the presidency.

KEY TAKE-AWAYS

- Lincoln and his party were greatly opposed to the Mexican-American War while others greatly supported it. Southern Democrats hoped to add more slave-owning territory at the war's end.
- Seward's and Chase's political careers were furthered during this time while Lincoln's political career became stalled.
- Lincoln's personal life was increasingly unhappy. His son Eddie passed away while his wife's sanity was slowly slipping.

CHAPTER 5: THE TURBULENT FIFTIES

Summary

The 1850s were a time of great turmoil, leading into the American Civil War. Congress had to decide whether the new territories acquired after the Mexican-American War would be slave-owning land or not. Politicians from throughout the country gave impassioned speeches both for and against this practice. Henry Clay was thought to be a savior for the nation. At 73 years old, Clay suggested letting California in as a state and allowing its legislature to determine its slave-owning status. He then suggested that New Mexico and Utah have no slavery restrictions. While he had hoped that the compromise would keep the Union together, many others were vocally opposed to these arrangements. Famous and impassioned speeches were given by John Calhoun, Daniel Webster, Seward, and Chase. Lincoln, who was reading about these goings-on through newspapers, gave himself over completely to the anti-slave movement. He and a number of others joined the newly created Republican Party, which was founded entirely on the notion that slavery was a great evil that should not be expanded. Specifically, the Republican Party spoke

against the Kansas-Nebraska Act, a bill
introduced by Stephen Douglas that allowed
Kansans and Nebraskans to decide the
fate of slavery in their states.

KEY TAKE-AWAYS

- The Republican Party was formed in 1854 by former-Whigs and abolitionists.
- Lincoln chose to devote himself to the anti-slavery movement.

CHAPTER 6: THE GATHERING STORM

Summary

The Nebraska Act passed in 1855 as Lincoln enjoyed his seat in the Illinois State Assembly. Lincoln also declared a run for the U.S. Senate, but his efforts were hampered by Mother Nature. A blizzard cut Springfield off from Illinois, which halted any quorums. Nearly a month passed between the storm and the February election. Lincoln lost, though he showed admirable humility and earned friends who would later help him during his presidential bid. At the time, however, Lincoln seemed to be at a standstill. He was forced to watch as the political arena rapidly changed. Democrats from the North defected, which gave Southern Democrats much more power. The Know Nothing Party was formed in order to fight against the granting of citizenship to immigrants and would later be called the American Party. Other smaller parties like the Fusion Party, the People's Party, and the Anti-Nebraska Party would also appear. The Whigs did not become the anti-slavery party as Lincoln had hoped. Instead, he jumped to the Liberty Party, the Free-Soldiers, and then became an independent Democrat before joining the Republicans. James

Buchanan won the presidency in 1856, near the same time the Supreme Court saw Dred Scott v. Sandford.

KEY TAKE-AWAYS

- Turmoil within parties was a significant development in the 1850s.
- The Dred Scott decision was yet another event that furthered the separation between Republicans and Southern Democrats.

CHAPTER 7: COUNTDOWN TO THE NOMINATION

Summary

Lincoln's strategy was fairly straightforward. He did not have a political manager, though he did put together an excellent staff to help guide his moves. He gave regular speeches that stirred thought and emotion. His staffers pushed for Chicago as the spot for the convention, which gave Lincoln the upper hand. Meanwhile, the three front-runners made costly mistakes that allowed Lincoln to move ahead. Seward chose to head overseas for eight months in order to avoid conflict at home. Upon his return, an old rival, newspaper editor Horace Greeley, wrote scathing pieces about Seward that chipped away at his reputation. Chase, meanwhile, made the assumption that he would gain the nomination during Seward's European sojourn. Chase rejected the idea of making political promises or using a campaign manager to secure votes. He turned down speaking addresses as well as forums, believing that well-written letters to journalists and others would suffice. The strongest issues for Bates were those with moderate Republicans. Bates was a powerful force with the Whigs but was deemed too conservative by many. He proved this even further by writing in a letter that "the Negro question" was only asked and answered by those who felt the need for "personal ambition or sectional prejudice." As he tried to ease his image, he only managed to isolate moderate Republicans and Southern Conservatives.

KEY TAKE-AWAYS

- Seward, Chase, and Bates made grave errors that would eventually cost them the nomination.
- Lincoln chose to speak in large venues that helped further his image even as few people considered him to be a viable candidate.

CHAPTER 8: SHOWDOWN IN CHICAGO

Summary

Lincoln and his handlers knew that he was not anyone's top choice for the nomination. However, he could easily step into the second-choice spot. This would give him a good chance at securing the nomination if one of the more politically seasoned men made a misstep. History shows that the mistakes made by Seward, Bates, and Chase were serious, though none of them felt so at the time. The convention in Chicago caused the city to become filled almost beyond capacity. Delegates filled hotels, boarding houses, and billiard halls. Once the convention started, a platform had to be decided upon as well as the requirements for securing the presidential nomination. Delegates chose a simple majority rather than a two-thirds rule for picking their favored nominee. Each man had representatives speak of his strengths while pouncing on opponents' weaknesses. Conversely, Lincoln chose not to speak ill of his competitors. Those who worked with him knew to follow suit. They felt that the other men would do all of the dirty work in pointing out the shortcomings of the competition while Lincoln and his handlers would focus their words on the thought that Lincoln would be able to deliver the presidency to the Republican Party.

KEY TAKE-AWAYS

• Lincoln made a decision to be a second-choice nominee for supporters of each of his competitors.
• Lincoln and his campaign workers seized on opponents' missteps not by focusing on their weaknesses but by focusing on Lincoln's strengths.

CHAPTER 9: A MAN KNOWS HIS OWN NAME

Summary

With the nomination secure, Lincoln then had to focus on gaining enough electoral votes to win the presidency. It was an uphill battle, with attacks Southern newspapers stating that he was ugly and illiterate. This would be countered with much success by the positive stories written by Republican journalists. He would need 152 electoral votes, which would not be an easy feat for the figurehead of a party that was newly formed and entirely based on anti-slavery values. Lincoln did not have a hope for winning any of the Southern states. Most did not include him on the ballot, though even if his name were present it was highly unlikely that he would get the necessary votes. Fortunately for Lincoln, the Democrats nominated two candidates: Stephen Douglas and John Breckenridge. The Constitutional Union Party also had a nominee in John Bell. These candidates would help to split the vote for Lincoln, which allowed him to carry those states he needed and then some. The last to announce returns was New York, whose 35 electoral votes took him over the top.

KEY TAKE-AWAYS

- The press played a large role in the election of 1860. Without the positive stories generated by Republican journalists, Lincoln likely would not have won the election.
- Lincoln's former rivals began to support him whole-heartedly. Seward traveled far and wide to give speeches; Bates wrote a published letter offering his support; and Chase spoke in Ohio, Indiana, and Michigan.

CHAPTER 10: AN INTENSIFIED CROSSWORD PUZZLE

Summary

Preparing to take office as a newly elected president, Lincoln had a road ahead of him that was arguably the most difficult in United States history. While many of his predecessors faced the nearly impossible task of creating a nation, Lincoln's job was to keep this nation held together in spite of vast differences. It was far more than a simple North vs. South fight. Lincoln's own party was conflicted as it was made from a number of warring factions in and of itself. He appointed Seward and Chase to his cabinet in the hopes that this would keep their supporters happy. Meanwhile, Southern Democrats were already gathering against the new president. On December 20, 1860, South Carolina decided to secede from the Union. James Buchanan, who would hold the presidency until Inauguration Day on March 4, had little effect on the efforts of South Carolina to hold onto the forts in its state.

KEY TAKE-AWAYS

- Through key appointments and grand gestures, Lincoln managed to keep the Republican Party held together during a time of great turmoil.
- Lincoln's predecessor, James Buchanan, had been ineffective at stopping the Civil War before it began.

CHAPTER 11: I AM NOW PUBLIC PROPERTY

Summary

Lincoln left Springfield for Washington with mixed emotions. He loved his adopted home and hoped to return. Rather than selling their home, the Lincolns chose to sell some of the contents, store others, and rent the house. On February 11, the Lincolns went to the train station in order to travel the distance to their new home. His speeches were always the cornerstone of Lincoln's character but had been bland since the presidential victory. Now, leaving Springfield, Lincoln left behind a memorable legacy and placed tears in the eyes of all who had gathered to watch him go, including his own. He said, in part, "To this place, and the kindness of these people, I owe everything." As the Lincolns journeyed, they traveled through various states where people had come to gather and meet the soon-to-be president. While the future first lady and her sons delighted at the spectacle, Lincoln worried about misconstrued appearances and possible assassination attempts. Indeed, Lincoln secretly ended his tour early, arriving in Washington before the crowds could attempt harm or speculation. He spent those days assembling his cabinet. He did so by compiling "former Whigs and Democrats." He picked men who would not simply agree with him but who would challenge his thoughts as well as each other's.

KEY TAKE-AWAYS

- Lincoln chose "the very strongest men" for his cabinet, regardless of their political backgrounds.

PART II: MASTER AMONG MEN
CHAPTER 12: MYSTIC
CHORDS OF MEMORY: SPRING 1861

Summary

Lincoln prepared his inaugural address with the aid of former rival Seward. Whereas Lincoln originally wanted a forceful address, meant to keep the Union together, Seward suggested a much softer approach. Though much of the address was somewhat easily changed, an area in which Seward felt trouble was a seeming reversal in stance on a proposed Constitutional amendment. Lincoln had previously encouraged and supported an amendment stating that "Congress could never interfere with slavery in the states where it already existed." He was now stating quite the opposite. At Seward's urging, Lincoln chose to return to his previous stance. Once given, Republicans said the speech was "admirable." Democrats called Lincoln "wretched" and "a fanatic." Upon his first day in office, Lincoln had to prove whether he was indeed admirable or wretched. He was given word from Major Anderson at Fort Sumter that provisions were near depletion. General Winfield Scott suggested surrender. Had Lincoln agreed to surrender, the following years could have been wildly different. After much discussion with experts and each Cabinet member, Lincoln chose to reinforce the fort. Southern troops fired upon Fort Sumter, and Anderson was forced to surrender in less than two days.

KEY TAKE-AWAYS

• Lincoln's first days in office were tumultuous at best. However, they allowed him to establish himself as a leader who would listen to and weigh the thoughts of those around him.
• Lincoln had made a "pledge to the North" to never abandon government property. By reinforcing Fort Sumter, he was not making a move toward war but was following through on one of his pledges.

CHAPTER 13: THE BALL HAS OPENED: SUMMER 1861

Summary

After the attack on Fort Sumter, the nation was truly divided and officially at war. Virginia soon seceded, which was followed by Tennessee, North Carolina, and Arkansas. Francis Blair, on Lincoln's behalf, asked Colonel Robert E. Lee to head up the Union troops. Lee told Blair that he viewed "secession as anarchy" but that he could not fight against his native Virginia. After some thought, Lee resigned from the Union Army. Lincoln also invited his brother-in-law, Benjamin Hardin-Helm, to become a major and paymaster in the Union Army. Like Lee, Helm chose to side with the Confederacy. Lincoln faced similar problems throughout these early days of war. The uncertainty and disagreements were compounded by fear from the general public. Meanwhile, Mary Lincoln took it upon herself to renovate the White House. She felt that restoring the White House would help to solidify the image of the federal government and, more specifically, the president himself. Unfortunately, her spending of thousands of dollars became newspaper fodder that only served to hurt the office. Another issue that Lincoln had to face was turmoil with would-be foreign supporters. It was thought that the British would side with the Confederacy in order to guarantee a continuous supply of cotton for their textile mills. With Lincoln's smooth maneuvering and Seward's aid, he was able to convince the British not to recognize the Confederacy as a sovereign nation. France soon followed. Still, the Union was faced with the hard task of financing a war that was being lost on the battlefield.

KEY TAKE-AWAYS

- The Union could not rely upon the best and brightest West Point graduates for their Army. Many were southerners who defected to the Confederacy.
- Lincoln's communication approach was of thoughtful resolve. He urged Northerners to remember the difficulties in putting the country together and the importance of unity.

CHAPTER 14: I DO NOT INTEND TO BE SACRIFICED: FALL 1861

Summary

Lincoln chose General George B. McClellan to lead the Union. McClellan was well-known and well-liked with the public and with troops. He was seasoned at training men, which would be necessary with the vast number of volunteers that would be needed during wartime. However, McClellan was arrogant and often showed his feelings of superiority to his commander-in-chief. Lincoln chose to overlook such slights as showing up late for appointments in order to have who he thought was the best man for the job. Unfortunately, McClellan did not prove himself to be thus. He was reluctant to engage the enemy, even at Lincoln's urging. Lincoln feared that McClellan would have to be replaced. Lincoln had also chosen Simon Cameron as the U.S. secretary of war. He was let go not long after and replaced by Edwin Stanton. Stanton proved to be an excellent choice in the role. He was an efficient leader and able to bypass the corruption that often took place in politics.

KEY TAKE-AWAYS

- The well-known General McClellan was thought by many to be the best leader during the Civil War.
- While McClellan was superior at training troops, he lacked the know-how to lead them into battle.

CHAPTER 15: MY BOY IS GONE: WINTER 1862

Summary

While the war was raging on, Lincoln's young son, Willie, contracted what was likely typhoid and eventually died. Both of the Lincolns were devastated, but Mary took it particularly hard. Lincoln had to spend a great deal of time with Mary to comfort her during her depression.

KEY TAKE-AWAYS

- The medical community was inept during the mid-19th century.
- Lincoln was able to handle very strong personalities, like Stanton's and his own wife's, even during times of great turmoil.

CHAPTER 16: HE WAS SIMPLY OUT-GENERALED: SPRING 1862

Summary

McClellan's promises of forward momentum left Lincoln with little hope. McClellan had yet to make serious movements during the war, and a bout with typhoid made Lincoln believe that McClellan was using his illness as a cover for not acting. Still, Lincoln felt it was his place to defer military judgments to those who were well-versed in the military. He listened as patiently as possible to McClellan but eventually issued his own battle plan. The strategy, which was put forth by Lincoln and generals under advisement, was to push the Rebels toward Richmond to shield Washington. Even with this new plan, McClellan did not act. He was ousted as general-in-chief on March 11 but continued to be in charge of the Army of the Potomoc. The general in chief role was left vacant while Lincoln, with Seward at his side, worked diligently to keep a balance in place. He visited McClellan in the field with the hope that a victory in Norfolk would help to end the fighting.

KEY TAKE-AWAYS

- McClellan was taken out of his position but continued to lead troops during the war.
- The "delays" caused by McClellan's inaction were thought to lead to a number of defeats, including the Seven Days Battle, which ended with 1,734 dead Union forces, over 8,000 wounded, and more than 6,000 missing or captured.

CHAPTER 17: WE ARE IN THE DEPTHS: SUMMER 1862

Summary

In 1862, it seemed as though the Union was bound to fail. Many of those in Lincoln's Cabinet as well as the general populace thought that a Northern victory was unlikely. Rather than admit defeat, Lincoln increased troop levels and restructured the military. Recruiting offices had been shuttered two months earlier and thus, to avoid a panic, Lincoln did not want to make a public plea for more volunteers. Instead, Seward worked with friends and colleagues to publicly draft pleas to the president to ask for more troops. Along with the increase in manpower, Lincoln appointed Henry Halleck as general in chief. The slavery question was also one that greatly needed to be answered. The president urged the legislature to pass a resolution that would encourage states to abolish slavery on their own rights. However, a resolution such as this met much consternation as many thought emancipation would lengthen the war. Bills were also passed to emancipate slaves in D.C. and to free fugitive slaves from the South.

KEY TAKE-AWAY

- With devastating losses, Lincoln and other Republicans focused on the legal issues surrounding slavery.

CHAPTER 18: MY WORD IS OUT

Summary

Lincoln's dismissal of McClellan did not immediately translate into a sudden turnaround for Northern forces. The Union lost significant battles at Chancellorsville and Second Bull Run. Indeed, desperation caused Lincoln to return to McClellan. Coincidentally or not, the Union saw a small victory at Antietam. Lincoln capitalized on this victory to share the Emancipation Proclamation.

KEY TAKE-AWAY

• Lincoln knew that the Emancipation Proclamation would be controversial. He chose to lead into emancipation by publicly stating that he neither sought to end or embrace slavery. He simply wished to save the Union. This angered many abolitionists who were unaware of the emancipation to come.

CHAPTER 19: FIRE IN THE REAR: WINTER-SPRING 1863

Summary

The president vowed to issue the Emancipation Proclamation on New Year's. Many naysayers thought that Lincoln's promise was empty rhetoric, meant to placate abolitionists in the face of a difficult war. Prior to the proclamation, several members of Lincoln's Cabinet had given input that he largely agreed upon and added to the final draft. Notably, Stanton and Chase urged Lincoln to include the proviso that freed blacks be entered into the armed forces. The proclamation was officially signed at about 10 p.m., forever changing the way the national government viewed slavery. The Emancipation Proclamation was celebrated by many, though there were those who worried that there was a political downside. However, any political backlash was secondary to the terrible loss at the Battle of Chancellorsville. The Union had hoped this would be a swift victory. The Army of the Potomac, led by Major General Joseph Hooker, was twice the size of General Stonewall Jackson's Confederate Army of Northern Virginia. Still, Jackson's troops managed to best the Union.

Seventeen thousand Union soldiers were killed. However, the Confederacy also saw major losses. They lost 13,000 men and suffered from another 13,000 casualties, and friendly fire led to the death of Jackson.

KEY TAKE-AWAY

• The Emancipation Proclamation was not solely Lincoln's work but was crafted with skillful thought and with the input of many of Lincoln's closest allies.

CHAPTER 20: THE TYCOON IS IN FINE WHACK: SUMMER 1863

Summary

Lincoln visited General Hooker on May 7, giving him the encouragement to head into another campaign. When he returned to Washington, he found that Clement Vallandigham, a congressman from Ohio, had been arrested and charged with treason. Vallandigham had loudly and publicly decried the war, which caused General Ambrose Burnside to arrest the man. When the *Chicago Times* spoke out against the act, Burnside forced the paper to close. Lincoln was in a quandary. He did not want to speak out against the general, but he also knew the political fallout of such an act could be enormous. In what was now typical fashion, Lincoln found a moderate approach. He commuted the sentence so that Vallandigham was banished to Tennessee, while publicly backing his general. The ban on the *Chicago Times* was also lifted. Lincoln did his best to settle the affair by having a letter published in the *New York Times*. The letter stated that military arrests were not allowed during "ordinary times," but that these extraordinary circumstances called for extreme measures. Lincoln likened

Vallandigham's language to desertion. Being the man who may cause soldiers to desert, and offense that was punishable by death, could be considered as grievous of a crime as any. The letter was widely praised. It may have been responsible for shifting public sentiment about Lincoln specifically and the war in general. However, not long after the publication of this letter, two key victories solidified the North's ability to come from behind to win the war. The Battle of Gettysburg was considered a turning point due to the massive number of rebel casualties. The same day that Gettysburg was declared victorious for the Union, July 4, General Grant led his own troops to victory at Vicksburg.

KEY TAKE-AWAYS

• Military force upon civilians was an unpopular but sometimes necessary part of the war.
• Victories at Gettysburg and Vicksburg marked the true turning point in America's Civil War.

CHAPTER 21: I FEEL TROUBLE IN THE AIR: SUMMER-FALL 1863

Summary

The summer of 1863 brought about many changes that would ultimately decide the outcome of the Civil War. They key change was Lincoln's choice to deploy black troops. This perhaps served to bolster those who were fighting for the Union. They saw these free blacks and former slaves as symbols for the war itself. It was also a reminder to southerners of all that they were faced with losing. The appearance of these men in Union uniforms may have been psychologically impactful during these long battles.

KEY TAKE-AWAY

- The deployment of all-black troops was no light matter. Even Lincoln himself had misgivings about arming black soldiers.

CHAPTER 22: STILL IN WILD WATER: FALL 1863

Summary

Edward Everett, former Harvard president, planned to give a speech at the site of the bloodiest battle of the Civil War. His address would serve as a dedication to the lives lost and those wounded during the Battle of Gettysburg. Lincoln would follow Everett with his own short speech, but with his busy schedule, he had precious little time to craft his words. Lincoln wrote the speech the evening before the event, giving Seward the chance to look it over before joining the procession. Everett's speech went on for two hours while Lincoln watched from the front row. The Gettysburg Address was only three paragraphs, but it was enough to leave the crowd speechless. It stated, in simple terms, the importance of a unified nation and the sanctity of those lost lives. After returning to Washington, Lincoln contracted smallpox. It was not a serious case, but he was still under forced bed rest. This gave him time to focus on Reconstruction.

KEY TAKE-AWAY

- The Gettysburg Address would become a fixture in history lessons for every generation after the Civil War. While it seemed that he had written the speech at the last moment, factually he had been crafting an address such as this for much of his political career.

CHAPTER 23: THERE'S A MAN IN IT!: WINTER-SPRING 1864

Summary

After several key victories, the Union was confident going into the holiday season. The Washington elite hosted a number of parties and receptions that were joyous occasions to all. However, the Lincolns could not enjoy their reverie for long. Many detractors took these events as opportunities to publicly blast the White House, often using slander and lies to spread vicious rumors about the pair. In the midst of all of this was the upcoming presidential race. Salmon Chase believed he had a chance at securing a nomination and even ousting the sitting president. Unfortunately for Chase, it seemed highly unlikely that anyone could beat Lincoln.

KEY TAKE-AWAY

• The Lincolns were not immune to public and private ridicule. However, this slander did not translate into a fear of the loss of the presidential office.

CHAPTER 24: ATLANTA IS OURS: SUMMER-FALL 1864

Summary

Lincoln wanted to renew hope in the troubled war. The Union had such high hopes of an imminent victory that they were now distraught about the stalemate they seemed to be suffering against the Rebels. He chose to speak at the Great Central Fair in Philadelphia, stating, "We accepted this war for an object, a worthy object, and the war will end when that object is attained. Under God, I hope it never will until that time." His words echoed and rang true. Lincoln continued to keep himself surrounded with the best possible cohorts he could find, even going so far as to accept a less-than-sincere resignation from Chase. However, his actions were not all met with open arms. The Wade-Davis Bill, an attempt at strict Reconstruction standards, was left unsigned on the president's desk. Lack of movement in battle as well as a raid on Washington made many of the Union supporters grow weary. Lincoln "desired" a second term. It appeared as though he would have some difficulty until two deciding factors came into play. First, the Democrats chose former General-in-Chief George McClellan as their candidate. Secondly, on September 3, Atlanta fell.

KEY TAKE-AWAY

• In a complete turnaround from the previous election, Lincoln seemed like an obvious choice for the presidency. However, if it were not for the excellent timing of the toppling of Atlanta, the outcome could have been different.

CHAPTER 25: A SACRED EFFORT: WINTER 1864-1865

Summary

Now on his path to becoming a second-term president, Lincoln was ready to face the nation head on. Though many thought he would rework his Cabinet, it mostly stayed the same. Lincoln had put together a true "team of rivals," men who would challenge him and each other in order to provide the best future for the nation. At this point, the future of the nation included the questions of slavery and citizenship for blacks. The Thirteenth Amendment had not passed in the House when it was brought before them the previous year. Lincoln asked them to debate the Amendment to abolish slavery once more. It took a great deal of effort and pressure to pass the Amendment through the House. Five Democrats were pressured to change their minds. Without them, the Amendment would not have gone through.

KEY TAKE-AWAY

• The Thirteenth Amendment was highly controversial. It passed by a narrow five-vote margin, which was arguably entirely arranged by Lincoln himself.

CHAPTER 26: THE FINAL WEEKS: SPRING 1865

Summary

After Lincoln's inauguration, he and his family traveled to visit Grant's headquarters at City Point. They met with their eldest son, Robert, who was now a captain serving under Grant. Lincoln met with Generals Grant and Sherman, hoping that more battles and bloodshed could be avoided. Unfortunately, it could not. The Third Battle of Petersburg was a northern victory that resulted in more than 7,000 casualties and deaths for both sides. General Lee retreated, leaving Confederate forces weakened and the Union ready to move in. This same day, General Grant captured Richmond. The war was effectively over. Only one month later, Generals Grant and Lee met at the Appomattox Court House to accept and tender the surrender of the Confederate Army, respectively. Only a few weeks later, Abraham Lincoln was dead from a gunshot wound to the head.

KEY TAKE-AWAY

• Along with the end of the war came great turmoil. Though the bloodshed was over, the entire country would have to work together to repair what had been so thoroughly damaged.

EPILOGUE

Summary

Vice President Andrew Johnson took over the role of president after Lincoln's death. Seward continued his work as Secretary of State, managed the purchase of Alaska, and then spent his remaining years traveling and spending time with his family. Bates stayed with family until he passed away at age 76. Before his passing, he had reconnected with his son, Fleming, who had joined the war effort for the Confederacy. Chase once more looked to vie for the presidency in 1868. Because Grant was running on the Republican ticket, Chase ran this time as a Democrat. He ran again in 1872 as a Liberal Republican but did not succeed in earning the nomination. Chase died at age 65. Mary and Tad returned to Illinois, where Tad died at the tender age of 18 and Mary was eventually placed in an asylum by her oldest son.

KEY TAKE-AWAY

- Each of the men who originally vied for the presidential nomination in 1860 went separate ways after Lincoln's death.

PUTTING IT TOGETHER

Through *Team of Rivals*, Doris Kearns Goodwin does not provide a typical historical narrative about the American Civil War. Instead, Goodwin helps the reader to understand why Lincoln chose to think the way he thought and act the way he did. Each of his choices was calculated in order to provide what he thought was the best chance for the country to recover through these long years of war.

Abraham Lincoln was not without fault. However, he was a man who wanted to do what was right. This led him to create allies where enemies once existed. This is displayed no greater than the deep friendship that developed between Lincoln and the favored candidate for the 1860 election, William Henry Seward. Lincoln also proved himself to be a forgiving man. He placed a southerner in his second-term cabinet. He also preferred to commute sentences and offer pardons than to force people into lengthy jail sentences or even executions. Though some argued that Lincoln pursued this public life because his private life was so lacking, others believe he did so out of a sense of responsibility to the country that allowed a simple country boy from rural Kentucky to become president of the United States.

Readers Who Enjoyed This Ebook Might Also Enjoy...

Doris Kearns Goodwin's *Team of Rivals* (the full book)

Candice Millard's *The River of Doubt*

Scott Miller's *The President and the Assassin*

Summary of Mark Owen's *No Easy Day: The Firsthand Account of the Mission That Killed Osama Bin Laden*

Made in the USA
Lexington, KY
28 November 2014